THE QUICK EXPERT'S GUIDE TO

Mobile Phone Photography

Janet Hoggarth

WAYLAND
www.waylandbooks.co.uk

First published in 2012 by Wayland

Wayland
338 Euston Road
London NW1 3BH

Wayland Australia
Level 17/207 Kent Street
Sydney, NSW 2000

Senior editor: Julia Adams
Design: Rocket Design (East Anglia) Ltd
Camera phone images: Janet Hoggarth, Nicola Markham
        and Neil Sheppard
All other images and graphic elements: Shutterstock

The author would like to thank the following people:
Number one, Nicola Markham whose talented pictures fill this
book. Number two Neil Sheppard for finding apps I never knew
existed and for all his geeky phone knowledge. Number three the
photographers and stylists I interviewed for on-the-job top tips:
Vicki Hillman, James Gillham, Ian Boddy, Ben Fisher. And finally
thanks to Emily Patel and Scott Boxall for being teenagers and
letting me bend their ears!

British Library Cataloguing in Publication Data
Hoggarth, Janet
Mobile phone photography. -- (Quick expert's guide)
  1. Photography--Digital techniques--Juvenile literature.
  2. Cell phones--Juvenile literature.
  I. Series
  771.3-dc23

ISBN 978 0 7502 7051 9

Printed in China

Wayland is a division of Hachette Children's Books,
an Hachette UK company

www.hachette.co.uk

>>>CONTENTS<<<

We have highlighted blogs, websites and tools throughout this guide in bold; we didn't want to overload you with URLs, but you should be able to find them really easily through search engines.

TO THE UTTERLY EXCELLENT WORLD OF MOBILE PHONE PHOTOGRAPHY!

So, you've got a phone. Useful for texting, ringing mates, ignoring calls from Mum and Dad asking what time you'll be home... AND taking pictures. But what do you do with your pictures? Do you look at them all the time and reminisce over what a great picture of beans on toast that was, or what an amazing picture of the back of Freya's head you took?

In which case, would you like to know a bit more about taking pictures on your phone? How to make them better? This excellent guide will show you just that. Get fistfuls of information on what effects to use and which apps to set your sights on; expert tuition on how to take good pictures; and brush up on your banter with the essential photographer vocab.

For the purposes of this book we are concentrating on the iPhone/iPod Touch, phones with the Android operating system and Blackberries. Otherwise the book would turn into a phone catalogue and we would all get confused. But of course all other types of camera phone are welcome!

FIRE UP YOUR CREATIVE FURNACE AND START FLEXING YOUR CLICK-FINGER FOR THE QUICK EXPERT TEAM'S SHOW-AND-TELL ON:

The **apps** that give your pictures that **extra zing**

Top tips for taking a **perfect** camera phone pic

The low-down on the **best** photo-sharing **websites**

Picture-taking **dos** and **don'ts**

The composition **tricks** of the professionals

SWITCHING ON YOUR INNER PHOTOGRAPHER

* BECOME FAMILIAR WITH YOUR CAMERA PHONE

Before you even start taking pictures, make sure you are familiar with the camera on your phone. All phones are different and some have a delay when you press the button. The iPhone only takes the picture when you take your finger off the button. Once you have fiddled about, and can work out what the delay is from pressing the button to the shutter closing, you will find taking pictures so much easier.

DIY DUDE
Let the picture-taking begin!

Right, you're not allowed to look at the rest of the book just yet. We're going to do a bit of a rookie's experiment to see how you cope without any top tips at the ready. Let's see if you can take some pictures based on what you think makes a good photo. Try taking some portraits of friends or family. If you can take a still-life of anything try that as well and endeavour to make it as interesting as possible without using any wizardry, just the lens on your camera and the lighting that you have available. Then you can compare the pictures you have taken now to the ones you will have expertly taken by the end of the book. Hopefully there will be a big difference!

A still-life is a composition of objects like fruit or plates — anything that doesn't move. The clue is in the name...

6

Dude!

✳ THE NUTS AND BOLTS

Before we go any further, we need to cover the basics. It's good to have an idea of what's going on inside a camera as you take the picture. Then you will appear super intelligent as well as being a complete photo-taking whizz.

The **lens** on a camera actually makes the picture. The most basic explanation is that it does this by collecting the light reflected from the subject that you are pointing it at and then focusing it on the surface of the film or sensor. There are all kinds of lenses: wide-angled, macro (very close up lens), zoom, telephoto, fish-eye. A lot of these are hard to fake with a camera phone, but some apps do allow for some sort of effect that may be similar to ones created by professional digital photography lenses. For example, some of the panorama effects are similar to wide-angled lens capture on a digital camera.

The **camera film** is the light-sensitive material behind the shutter in a traditional camera. The film is exposed when the shutter on the camera opens, flooding the film with light and capturing the image you have just pointed the lens at. Of course there are whole books on different films — it is worthy of that kind of investigation if you want to go down the serious photography route.

Instead of film in a digital camera or camera phone, there is an **image sensor**. In basic terms this is a device that converts the light coming through the camera lens into an electric signal ready to be processed by the camera's computer, which will then turn that into an optical image.

The **aperture** is the hole inside the camera lens that with adjustment manually or digitally allows light through to the sensor/film.

The **shutter** is a device that allows light to pass through the aperture on the lens for a period of time, in order to expose photographic film or a light-sensitive electronic sensor to light and capture an image.

Shutter delay is when there is a lag between pressing the shutter button and the camera actually taking the picture. It is a bit of a problem when taking pics on your camera phone! (See page 18 on how to sort this one out.)

Shutter speed in a nutshell is how quick or slow the shutter is on a Digital Single Lens Reflex (DSLR) or Single Lens Reflex (SLR) camera. A quick shutter speed lets in less light onto the digital sensor or film if it is a DSLR or SLR camera and vice versa. As with a lot of these terms, you won't need to know that as there is no shutter speed on a camera phone and no shutter. It just takes the picture when you press the button.

A **filter** in the world of photography is a transparent piece of tinted glass, plastic or gelatine used to alter the colour or character of light or to reduce the amount of light. The whole appearance of the photo can be changed dramatically by changing filters. In digital photography this can be done on a computer using Photoshop or something similar. A lot of the camera photo apps are lots of different filters that effectively 'slide' over the top of the photo you have taken on your phone.

A fish-eye lens is a lens that distorts the image to appear like a fish would

>> THE BOFFIN BIT <<

PIXELS SCHMIXELS

A pixel is a small dot in a digital photography image. Thousands of pixels make up a digital photograph. When someone says a picture is pixelated, it means it is of such poor quality that you can actually see the dots from which the picture is made. Not a good look! Resolution is a measure of the number of pixels there are on a digital camera sensor or a digital photograph. So a pixilated picture would be a low resolution photograph and a sharp, good quality one would be high resolution. The resolution of digital cameras is measured in megapixels – millions of pixels: the higher number of megapixels your camera phone has, the higher the resolution of its pictures.

see the world — completely wide angled and sometimes totally spherical. You can get non-spherical lenses, too. Some phone camera apps have these lenses available to shoot through on your camera phone, or they manipulate the image so it looks like it has been shot that way.

✳ JUST POINT AND SHOOT, RIGHT?

Well, no not really! If you want some excellent pics there are two things you need to think about as you get ready to take that shot: light and how to focus.

✳ Think about lighting

If you can get the lighting of the pic right you are pretty much sorted. There are various lighting issues you need to think about. **Backlighting** is when the subject of a photo is lit from behind — pretty self-explanatory! But if you have no backlighting available, there are apps that can fake it for you.

Exposure occurs when light is allowed to strike a digital camera's image sensor or a traditional camera's film, so when the sensor/film is exposed to light. It can also be explained as the total amount of light striking the sensor/film or other photographic material from a combination of shutter speed and aperture used in exposing the sensor/film in a camera. **Proper exposure** refers to a particular exposure that produces an image that is in every way perfect to the photographer. Photos can be **underexposed**, which is when there is no difference between the shadows and the picture can be very dark. **Overexposed** pictures are when the photos are washed out white (blown out) because too much light has flooded the sensor/film. Brain implosion, anyone?

Lens flare happens when you shoot directly into the light source and it can be like a bright flash of light in the picture (like a white orb) or, if the light source is just out of shot, it can cause a general washed out look in your picture. It can be accidental or intentional. There are effects you can add on afterwards to make it look like your picture has lens flare, and they can change the atmosphere of the picture entirely.

✳ Think about how to focus

Now you've sussed out lighting, you need to think about what you want to focus on within the image, and how. **Depth of field** is a measure of how much of a scene (from the front to the back of the image) will be in focus. If you're shooting a landscape photo you probably want everything in focus, from a tree in the foreground to the hills in the distance (deep depth of field). For portrait photography it's usually best to have a shallow depth of field (i.e. keep only part of the image in focus). This allows the subject to be in clear focus, but makes the background blurred. All you need to know is that depth of field is mostly controlled by the aperture of the lens. There are apps to help blur backgrounds to fake all these real-time digital photography effects.

Bokeh refers to the blur, or more specifically, the quality of the blur in out-of-focus areas of a photograph. Generally it is considered good practice, especially with portrait photography, to have the main subject in focus and the background blurred. Bokeh is subjective really and everyone has their own preference about how evenly and pleasingly the out-of-focus (blurred) area looks. This photo has been tampered with in an app to fake the bokeh round the subject, making her face stand out.

✳ WHEN IT ALL GOES WRONG!

Obviously your photos never go wrong... well, not exactly, but it's good to know what can go wrong so you can try to avoid it! **Red-eye** is the term for the unwelcome effect caused by light from a flash travelling through the iris and illuminating the retina at the interior back of the eye (which is red in colour from the blood vessels there — yuk). The camera then captures that redness on film or on a digital camera's sensor. If you use the flash on your phone (assuming there is one) you may have to go and use an edit suite to eliminate red-eye afterwards, if you are bothered by it.

Blown out is a term used to describe the over exposure of a shot where the picture can appear very white; see the explanation on page 9 on exposure!

When photographers mention **noise** they mean the small coloured blotches, usually in the darker areas of an image that appear on a digital photograph. Noise often goes overlooked in snapshots, but becomes very obvious if enlargements are made. A better-quality camera produces less noise. Film grain on old-school film is considered attractive and cool and is the film equivalent, but noise isn't cool. So digital photographers will start with a noise-free image and add grain on afterwards in an edit suite. Obviously there are apps that mimic this grainy effect.

CAMERA PHONE FACT

The word photography is formed from two Greek words: photos (light) and graphein (to draw), and was first used in the 1830s.

* A WORD ON EFFECTS

Now you've considered the importance of light, how to focus and what pitfalls to avoid, you can think about the fun stuff: the effects! Some of these terms are names of filters that are available at your fingertips in the app store for your phone. Sometimes a bit of background knowledge can be helpful so you can decide what effect might be best for what kind of photo. Edit suites are brilliant apps that can change all sorts of aspects of your camera phone photo.

Cross-processing is a back-in-the-day film term. It refers to the practice of deliberately developing film in chemicals intended for a different type of film. For example, developing a slide film using print film chemicals. The result is unnatural colours and contrasts. There are filters and apps that can recreate this type of look.

High Dynamic Range Imaging (HDRI or **HDR)** can give stunning results. In the world of digital photography, HDR images combine two or more images which are identical apart from having different exposures. It means that the image contains all the range of colours and light and shade, making it an intense experience. Some people find these techniques too painterly, but everyone has an opinion in photography! There are apps out there that fake this effect (not very well) and edit suites that can actually do it for camera-phone photography. The iPhone has a setting built in for HDR that takes three different pictures and blends them for a better quality. But none are anywhere near as good or effective as real HDR photography with a DSLR camera.

Tilt shift is a brilliant effect that you will get hooked on. Before photo edit suites and wizardry, you would have had to purchase a special lens to do this. Using the effect on your phone, you can blur the foreground and the background so the picture has a small depth of field. This tricks your eyes into thinking that the image is of a subject that is quite close to your eyes, and so must be small. Have a go later on, when we get to the app section, and try it for yourself!

Vignetting is a term you will come across a lot during phone photography if you use filters and effects. Vignetting is when the edges of the photo are faded or burnt out to the outer rim of the picture causing the middle of the photo to really stand out, as in the example here of a seaside scene. The focus really is drawn to the centre of the picture away from the vignette frame.

Monochrome is a term for an image of a single colour in differing shades. A black and white or sepia-toned image is a monochrome.

Panning technique involves taking a picture while moving the camera. It is almost always used when tracking a moving object as it travels across the film plane. When properly carried out, the object is rendered relatively sharply while its surroundings are blurred.

>> THE BOFFIN BIT <<

HISTOGRAMS

Now the word Histogram is going to flash before your eyes if you download an edit suite onto your phone (see chapter 4) or use an online one. The simplistic way of explaining a histogram is that it is a graph that displays where all of the brightness levels contained in the scene you are photographing are found, from the darkest to the brightest. These values are arrayed across the bottom of the graph from left (darkest) to right (brightest). The vertical axis (the height of points on the graph) shows how much of the image is found at any particular brightness level.

On a normal digital camera this graph will be displayed on the screen near the view finder. If you use an edit suite to change the contrast in a digital camera phone photo, making it lighter or darker, you are tinkering with the histogram reading and altering the balance between light and dark. Of course it is way more in-depth than that and way, way more technical, but you don't really need to know that for this type of book. Just keeping you in the loop!

✳ OH, THE POSSIBILITIES

Camera phones are awesome for taking spur-of-the-moment pics but you may want to explore other possibilities. Toy Cameras are a fun alternative, or you could venture out further into the world of photography and save up for a more professional digital camera with which to continue your journey into taking cool pictures.

☀ Toy Cameras

Toy Cameras are a family of cheap cameras that were developed in China and Russia as a point-and-press camera for the masses. There's no manipulation of the focus or aperture — it is all fixed. They are typically manufactured out of plastic, including the lens. These cameras can give really cool results, such as vignetting round the edges of photos, super bright colours, light streaks and blurring. They are considered very artistic and a whole Toy Camera movement has a strong presence in the photographic world. Check online to find out more information. Apps can recreate artistic photos from all the Toy versions that are out there including the Holga, Lomo (lots of different cameras under this umbrella), Diana and Pinhole cameras.

☀ SLR/DSLR

SLR stands for Single Lens Reflex and is a design of camera where the photographer looks straight through the lens prior to taking a photograph. The view through the viewfinder of a SLR camera is therefore the exact same image that will be recorded by the camera. Simple. A DSLR is a Digital Single Lens Reflex camera, where you can view the image that will be recorded by the camera on a screen and is what most professional photographers use today.

QUICK EXPERT SUMMARY

- ◉ Get to know everything about your camera phone, all its little oddities and don't be scared of pressing buttons and finding stuff out.

- ◉ Know how to look after your camera phone. Get a protection case and a proper microfibre cloth to wipe the lens clean.

- ◉ Experiment with how to take a picture! Light and how to focus are key.

- ◉ If you have a heads-up on what different effects mean and where they originate from, you can apply them more professionally and be able to talk about your creations like an expert.

TIPS TO IMPROVE YOUR PICTURES

Anyone can tart up a basic point-and-press photo with filters and apps. But isn't it best to start off with a really well-crafted photo and turn it into something vastly interesting using the technology you have at your fingertips?

SAY WHAT?

> If I'm shooting location references or model headshots or just to aid memoires then I want the pictures to be honest so I don't tend to enhance them in any way.
>
> **Ian Boddy, Photographer**

✳ TAKING PICTURES OF PEOPLE

Try to avoid direct sunlight so your friends don't have sunlight blinding them and lighting them fairly shockingly (they won't thank you for it. Every zit will be on show!). Overcast is the best light and most flattering. If it is sunny get them to stand/sit in the brightest part of the shade so they aren't overexposed. When photographing adults, experiment with both the angle of your composition and the angle of light to see what's most flattering: taking a picture from above or below makes for a more interesting result, as you can see in this picture. It's easier with adults from below as they have a longer body and the effect can be more dramatic. It doesn't mean you can't do this with kids though! Just try all sorts of different angles, see what looks good. With small kids and animals try getting down on their level or lying alongside.

A camera phone isn't able to isolate the subject of the picture from the background. You have two options to deal with this. You can either go with less clutter as in the first picture, and make sure your subject is in front of a simple background, or simply fill the image with the person or the object you are photographing, as in the second picture. This works well for any subject in a busy background/poor lighting situation.

SAY WHAT?

> " *Fashion photographers shoot low for a good perspective, so try shooting from below. A fashion photographer would never shoot high.* "

**Vicki Hillman,
Fashion Stylist**

*KEEPING IT STEADY

Hold the camera phone with both hands and brace your upper arms against your body when you shoot, keeping it as close to your body as possible. Don't take your photo while you're actively breathing. Wait until you hit the shutter button before you exhale! (Don't take too long to press or you might pass out.) However, the best way to snap a non-blurry camera phone photo is to anchor your arm or elbow on a rigid surface, such as a table or window frame.

Shutter delay is a big cause of blurry pics. On camera phones and all point-and-press digital cameras, there is a delay between the release of the button on the phone and the time that the light actually hits the sensor. That's when you could mess it all up and cause a blurry photo and ruin your chance of catching the perfect moment. Holding the camera really steady, even after the button has been pressed, for a few extra seconds more can help reduce jelly pics. If you want to take it one step further and go major league pro, some camera apps also aim to help counteract the effect of shaking. iPhone users can use Camera Plus Pro, an app which includes an anti-shake image stabiliser among many other features. Android users can opt for the popular app Camera360, which features a similar stabiliser, see page 47).

> *Use the rule of thirds (put the subject in a third of the picture) and don't use the flash. Hold the phone against a wall to hold it steady; there is always a natural tripod around somewhere.*

Photographer James Gillham's top tips for taking great pictures

✳ WHAT CAMERA SETTINGS TO CHOOSE

You might want to fiddle with your actual camera phone settings. Some have options for portrait, landscape, night-time, movement and so on. Some camera phones, even really basic ones, have a setting for taking panoramic pictures by knitting several pictures together — this can be really cool if you want to do a cityscape or landscape picture. If you are shooting at night, some camera phones allow a longer exposure so more light can hit the sensor. Try taking different pictures on different settings. Mix it up a little. Experiment with the actual hardware of your phone. You might be able to create some cool pictures without getting an effect anywhere near it! This picture was taken on a basic Samsung non-smartphone without apps. The panorama stitch effect was found in the settings! Pretty impressive.

* LIGHTING TIPS

Your light source should be behind you when you take the picture, as already discussed when taking pictures of people. Experiment with the flash. A lot of photographers aren't a fan of the flash. Most phones have a flash that can be turned off or on. See what effect you can get by putting the flash on when it's not needed, or turning it off when the phone wants to use it.

It's always best to try and use a natural light source if you can. Of course we aren't always shooting outside in natural sunlight (disco in the morning anyone?), so why not cheat using a desk lamp, table lamp or good old-fashioned torch? See what kind of effects these give. The iPhone has a backlight illuminated sensor that is supposed to improve dark conditions; but if you haven't got an iPhone just make the most of what you have got around you.

This night-time picture uses the bridge's overhead light as the main light source taken on a basic phone camera with no fancy apps. Instead we switched it to night-setting to let in more light. Not all smartphones have a night-setting though, which is why some older phones have better night-time picture-taking ability. You've got to keep that hand steady though; letting in more light leaves more room for error meaning blurry pictures.

> ❝ A backlight is always good. Have a light behind and get your friend's head to cover it. If you want flare, get them to move their head slightly and let a bit of light come through. ❞
>
> *Vicki Hillman, Fashion Stylist*

With natural photography like land and seascapes wait for the 'magic hour' and harness the natural light source in front of you. The 'magic hour', during the times of sunrise and sunset, is when the sky is colourful enough for even a camera phone to capture land and sky with fairly good exposure.

With street photography and natural photography, be aware of your lighting, but you don't necessarily have to follow the rules of the sun behind you. Depending on the mood you're aiming for, sometimes taking a photo facing directly into the sun can give you interesting results. You can end up with lens flare which can be cool and atmospheric. Give it a go. In this picture the skyscraper partially blocks the sun causing a suggestion of lens flare.

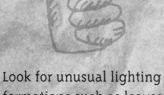

Look for unusual lighting formations such as leaves dappling the sunlight, if you are outside. Shoot from under the dappling or into the dappling light and see what effects you can achieve. Shooting straight into the sun here through a tree has caused full-on lens flare, creating a flower effect.

Capturing shadows of people/objects/structures can also be a more interesting way of taking a less conventional picture. With this picture of the London Eye, the photographer has chosen to take a picture of the shadow cast by the wheel rather than the wheel itself. Also, look at a bright sunny day from inside by shooting out into a street scene or a garden, for example. You can create interesting contrasts.

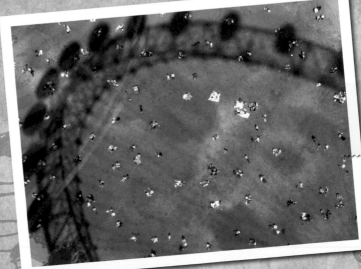

✳ AVOID USING THE ZOOM

Digital zoom is deceiving, and some phones don't even come with the feature. All digital zoom does is enlarge the image rather than zoom in, and so it immediately becomes pixelated (see page 8). If you can, it's best to avoid using it, and instead simply move closer to your subject. Of course that isn't going to help if you're at a gig trying to get up close and personal with your rock god on the stage! Maybe get more expensive seats next time...? However, there is a free app for the iPhone called Camera Zoom that you could experiment with if you have an iPhone or an iPod Touch. But to be honest, it really isn't that much better.

This is loads of fun! Get a friend to jump on a skateboard/bike/rollerblades or just run very fast. Grab your phone and hold it steady against your body and pan (move) the camera to follow your friend at roughly the same speed they are going (hopefully not at the speed of light). Take the picture mid-pan. In theory you should get a clear picture of them frozen in motion with the background blurred. I said in theory. It takes a lot of practice and they have to be going fast!

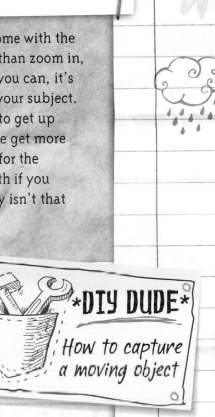

DIY DUDE

How to capture a moving object

Dude!

* COMPOSITION TIPS

This section could muscle in and take over the whole book if we're not careful! There are literally so many tips you can utilise to instantly improve your photo-taking ability that we may have to reign ourselves in to stop getting too overexcited! Composition is the way you choose to arrange the subjects in your photos. Some people are born knowing how to do this, and some of us are rubbish! Chopping heads off, random hands and feet getting in the frame, a picture of the table instead of the people sat around it — sound familiar? These guidelines are used by photographers to create a pleasing composition. But, as we know, all rules are made to be broken...

The rule of thirds

The rule of thirds technique refers to dividing the scene into thirds vertically and horizontally and placing the subject on one of the dividing lines. This is the most famous composition guide. Lots of photographers refer to it when asked to impart wisdom on taking good photos. The idea of putting a subject slap-bang in the middle of a picture isn't a pleasing composition. Placing it off-centre makes for a more attractive picture. Check out the pictures below and see what you think. Situating Big Ben left of centre has more effect than it would if it was right in the middle. However, some subjects just work centrally. Parallel lines and symmetrical shapes disappearing into the distance can sometimes look better if placed centrally in the frame. Here, the skeleton looks great in the centre.

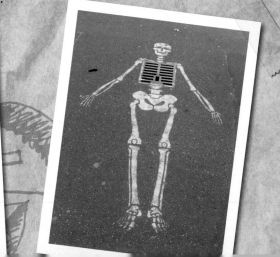

When you are implementing the rule of thirds it works best if your subject is facing into the picture rather than out of it. And, if you are capturing a moving object it's good to give that object (taxi cab, person walking along the street, errant pet cat, gerbil...) space to travel into the picture so you can see their potential direction of travel. The train is travelling into the picture here and we can still see where it has to go.

The iPhone and iPod Touch have the grid lines available on the camera if you switch them on. And a lot of apps have them too as a guide for composition. But as already stated, just placing the subject left of centre will do just that. Have a play around. Take a picture of your friend, bowl of bananas, plate of spaghetti, Mum, a tree, a pizza, whatever you fancy right in the middle of the photo. Then take a picture with your chosen subject off-centre and see the difference.

Dude!

Leading lines, diagonals and curves

Leading the viewer's eye into the picture is another composition trick utilised by photographers. You can use anything of interest like a repeated row of fence posts or boats lined up in a marina, and more solid lines like a path or string of fairy lights and a row of washing. Leading lines can be diagonals, curves or different forms. Setting the subject on a diagonal can be a striking way of presenting a different image. Move around the subject you are trying to capture and make a diagonal if you can. Also look out for symmetrical lines and shapes that balance each other.

The curve of the table echoes the circle on the pavement behind in this example.

The line of boats draws the viewer into the picture from the edge of the photo.

On this Parisian bridge our eyes are drawn diagonally across the picture while at the same time taking in the intricate detail of the thousands of padlocks clamped onto the railings.

Contrasting textures and surface

Look out for different textures when taking pictures as these can make interesting photos, especially if you photograph two or more different ones together and get quite close in to really see the surfaces of them.

Framing and cropping

Photographers use unconventional framing to create a unique picture. For example, shooting through an arch or using trees to break up the skyline can be effective. Try and find a frame that works for you. Anything could be a frame. Coming in really close and capturing details rather than the complete image can make a more fascinating picture. This is called cropping. Sometimes photographers do this afterwards by blowing up photos and cutting parts out. You can do this on an iPhone or other smartphones. Go into your settings and check if you have a cropping option because then you can take a photo, blow it up and crop it but keep the original picture as well. The detail of the New York fire hydrant is intriguing because you can't tell what it is immediately.

Landscape and scenery photography

A cool tip when trying out landscape, sunset or sunrise pictures is to try and get the horizon in the natural place; low down in the picture. Sometimes putting the horizon down low dramatises the sky above making a lovely composition.

QUICK EXPERT SUMMARY

- Composition of a photo is key.
- Work on placing the focus of the picture in different thirds of the photo to get alternative reproductions of the same object without using any filters or anything flash.
- Adjust angles, closeness to the subject, lighting. It will be a good way for you to work out how different elements, other than just pointing and pressing, can affect a subject.
- Master the art of taking a good picture before you start experimenting. Get the basics sorted and soon you will be ready to move on to adding all the jiggery pokery of filters and effects.

SHOW AND TELL

Let's take a quick look at some photos that work and don't work to help you on your journey to becoming an expert photographer.

* FLASH BANG WALLOP, WHAT A PICTURE

It takes no time at all to just observe what you are looking at in order to improve any picture you are about to take. All professional photographers do this. Unless they are the paparazzi trying to get a picture of David Beckham coming out of the loo! So, for instance, next time you are at a party and want to capture the essence of how the event is going down, do a recce first; walk round, check it out, look for the interesting people, anything funny going on, keep your camera ready to go at any moment so you can capture as quick as a flash.

Remember, the action actually might be at the edge of the party, so check out, through your lens (scan the room with the camera on, finger on the button ready!), to see if you can catch anything way more interesting than someone spilling yet another drink down Alice's top. What's happening just out of the frame of where you are trying to photograph? You never know, you could strike gold. Observe, observe, observe.

> ❝ *I think the best pictures are often on the edges of any situation; I don't find photographing the situation nearly as interesting as photographing the edges.* ❞
>
> **William Albert Allard,**
> **The Photographic Essay**

In this portrait you can see how harsh sunlight creates dark shadows and is very unflattering.

The next picture reveals too much space above the subject, though the lighting is much more preferable, being shot in the bright shade instead.

The final picture is the most pleasing as we are close in to the subject and the frame is filled with the subject looking into the picture. The lighting is balanced and flattering and there are no over-dramatic shadows or harsh bleached out white spots.

DIY DUDE

Stunt photography

Set an old camera phone (unless you are confident about your catching ability) to timer, if it has that option, throw your phone up in the air and see what sort of picture you get! Poor man's aerial photography! Or take pics while on rollerblades or skateboard and snap away. From the window of the car is possible too, but it isn't as much fun!

Dude!

This shot is a great picture but it doesn't quite work because of the tiny reflection of the other building on the left-hand side. A clean line would have been preferable.

The photographer moved the camera just slightly and eradicated the other reflection creating a better composition, with clean lines shooting up to the top of the skyscraper. This also breaks the rule of thirds with the reflection slap bang in the middle of the frame because the symmetrical lines either side draw your eye upwards towards the horizontal cut-off point of the top of the building.

Another example of the lines drawing you into a picture is this photo utilising the road markings as an arrow to bring your eye to the New York yellow cab just at the top of the photo. It is also illustrating using the rule of thirds by placing the cab not quite in the centre at the top making the photo much more engaging than the next example of the same stretch of road.

This picture taken at a different angle doesn't work because the parallel lines aren't centrally hooking you in and there is no subject at the top of the photo for your eyes to focus on. It's a bit of a nothing!

SAY WHAT?

" A lot of camera phone shots are too dark in the foreground because the background is bright and the camera is auto-exposing for this. On an iPhone, tap and hold an area of the screen showing the foreground, until a blue square flashes, which locks the exposure and focus. Try it; you will get correctly exposed foregrounds/subjects with nice blown-out backgrounds. Lovely. "

Ian Boddy, Photographer

This landscape picture isn't totally rubbish, but it could be a lot better! There is too much greenery and the bushes and trees aren't really super interesting. What is interesting is the city in the background but it is swamped by the unruly foliage and instead of noticing the city we are drawn to the dark shadowy gap in the trees in the middle of the picture.

This photo is much better. By moving the horizon lower down in the frame, the city is the focus of the picture with the clouds drawing you down from the top right-hand corner to the more natural horizon line almost at the bottom of the composition. The tree in the bottom left also echoes the large cloud in the top right. And the photo creates strong horizontal lines from the foliage, to the city, to the clouds. A much more pleasing photo!

CAMERA PHONE FACT

On 17 January 2007, New York City Mayor, Michael Bloomberg, announced a plan to encourage people to use their camera phones to capture crimes happening in progress and send their video or pictures directly to the police. Wow! When in NYC, you'd better be on your best behaviour then. No messing!

Why camera phones are the way forward

"I do have a separate camera but I don't use it because it's extra stuff to carry when you're going out. So, I think phones are the best because I always have it with me."

Emily, age 13

QUICK EXPERT SUMMARY

- The three major things you must do before you take a picture: Stop. Think. Look.

- Observe what you are looking at and remember, the action may be at the edge of the party.

- Some of the best pictures are when people are caught unawares and not putting on their 'photo-ready' face! Catch them looking away from the camera.

- Expert, expert, expert! You're never off duty!

IT'S ALL IN THE APP

This is the bit that you have all been waiting for, the wizardry, the Harry Potter moment of glory. You are about to turn your innocent snap into a world-beating, prize-winning image that will be used in the next Nike campaign or at least, be envied by all your mates. Right, let's get on and see if we can have you having an app-off with your friends. Our app's better than yours...

✳ SO, APPS AWAY...

If you have grown up in a cave and have just recently made it out into the world, you may not know what a phone is, let alone a camera phone or indeed an iPhone, never mind what an app is. Quick recap: an app is short for application, an added extra that you can download from the app store (there is an app store for all smartphones including iPhones/iPod Touch, Android phones and Blackberry phones). Photo apps are great fun and you can really have a major experiment with them.

A lot of the effects are just filters like you would put over the lens on a manual SLR (Single Lens Reflex) camera (back in the day!) or give you a picture similar to using a Toy Camera with special film (for example the Lomo camera and the Polaroid black and white camera). All these filters and different camera lenses and effects can change the colour of pictures, and make it look like a dream or an antique photo. Pictures can look washed-out, colour saturated, or have vignetting, to add a different feeling and atmosphere to just a simple snap.

There are edit suite apps available where you can tweak pictures even more by changing the gradient of the colour on the picture after taking the shot. You are in control of the washed-out version of your picture and it's not a filter or a one-stop effect, you are creating the complete look! You might want to enhance the focus of a picture and hone in on one aspect of it, leaving the rest of the picture out of focus, something that in the real world of photography means buying an expensive lens to achieve. Well, using a spot-focus app or tilt-shift app can do that for you. There's nothing to stop you taking really amazing photographs without having to spend all the money you have in the world on lenses. A lot of these apps are free or cost a small amount, about the same as a can of Coke. So, are you ready to unleash your creativity and try out some apps?!

✳ DON'T WORRY ABOUT WHAT PHONE YOU HAVE

Here we are, making the mad assumption that you have an iPhone in the first place. You probably don't. But you may have an iPod Touch, or an Android phone, which also has an app store all of its own. Maybe you have a Blackberry; a lot of kids do as it has the free text messaging service that you all love to use day and night, secretly under the school desk. Sadly, there are only a few decent photo apps for these BUT, you may have filters and effects built into your phone in the camera function itself. Or you could have a basic camera phone with no flashing lights, filters or impressive show-off applications. What you may have is a lead (if you haven't lost it) allowing you to transfer all your pictures onto a computer so you can store them safely and then upload them to sites that allow you to showcase your pictures and edit them with a few effects, too.

We have an old basic phone but it has all sorts of camera settings. We've taken some great photos, some of them in this book, and then added filters and effects on afterwards either in the built-in edit suite or on an online one.

✳ WHAT'S AVAILABLE?

Now, there are so many camera apps for the Android and for the iPhone that if you downloaded every single one, as well as all your games, pictures, other apps, your phone might have a meltdown and stop working. There is only so much space for everything to fit. This book obviously only just skims the surface of what is available in the photo app world, so you must go out there and see for yourself. Just because it says it is a photography app doesn't mean you will need it and it will be any good, so this is meant as a very condensed guide to start you off. And, as always, the best place to get started is with the free ones. Some of the good ones will have offers where they are free for a limited period of time. So snap these up if you see them for free in your app store.

There seem to be two camps for using these apps in the professional world of photography: those who do use apps and those who don't, and prefer the clean image. There's nothing wrong with either camp; everyone is allowed an opinion. Have an experiment and see what you prefer.

SAY WHAT?

❝ I use my iPhone to take pictures all the time but I never use the effects apps. I like to have the pure image, although I love it when other people take pictures with effects. ❞

James Gillham, Photographer

✳ IPHONE APPS

Let's start with the original app store and work down. You may have an iPod Touch which is the iPhone without the huge phone bills. You can still access all the apps for the camera because the camera is the same as the one in the iPhone. We also assume all of you know how to download an app from the store.

GET REAL! What's your favourite app?

"I do have a separate camera but Instagram is much cooler."

Scott, age 13

Instagram

This is the best free app you will find for your iPod Touch or iPhone. It's not as broad creatively as some of the other apps because there is no exposure adjustment or tweaking of the creative filters it applies. But it still has some cool old-school filters and a great spot focus that lets you home-in on a section of your chosen picture and blur the surrounding area so that one part of the picture is sharp as a knife and really stands out. If applied in a certain way to pictures taken from a distance so the subjects are quite small, you can create photos that look like fake model miniatures. This is called a tilt-shift effect (see page 43).

What's also great is that you can take pictures you have already taken on your phone, put them in Instagram and apply filters afterwards. This way you are always left with a clean original copy and multiple effects copies as well. You can upload to the Instagram photo-sharing site from inside the app as well as other well-known photo-sharing sites. The site has a feed so you can follow certain people, like on **Twitter**, and see what photos they're taking. It's good to see how other people interpret the world!

You can see the difference Instagram makes by looking at these two pictures. The original untampered version and then the photo with a filter washing it out slightly, with spot focus over the little girl. This small edit makes for a more dramatic picture improving a basic photo and turning it into something very atmospheric.

Darkroom

Darkroom is free and only takes the picture when your hand is steady. This is perfect if you are constantly taking pictures in low light. Darkroom's steady mode feature takes a photo automatically once there's no movement. You'll only need to focus on the subject and keep your hands steady.

Facebook Camera

Facebook Camera is a relatively new contender in the arena of apps but worth mentioning because it is free and we know what a load of **Facebook** addicts you all are! Currently it is only iPhone compatible but hopefully it will be there for you all to use very soon. It's a camera that directly downloads the photos you take to Facebook as well as the added joy of filters and a basic editing suite too. Possibly aimed at more mainstream snappers than anyone wanting to really shake things up.

Lego Photo

This is a fun app which converts your photo into **Lego** bricks — hilarious! It's free and is rather hit-and-miss, but if you take the right image it can really work. It needs lots of experimentation and works best with faces.

SAY WHAT?

❝ Using the iPhone as a camera makes me more creative. ❞

Ben Fisher, Photographer

✳ Photosynth

This is possibly the coolest app for mega pictures! And it is free, so a bonus. Basically, you can take 360° pictures using your iPhone or iPod Touch and the app stitches them together creating a dynamic interactive picture that you can move around with your finger on the screen and look at from all angles. It's great for taking awesome shots from high up, landmarks and scenes where you just want to capture all the action going on without missing a single shot. If you want the pictures to conform to a traditional shape (they can look haphazard depending on how you shoot them), you can easily crop using the cropping tool in the camera phone settings, or afterwards in an edit suite. You can upload from the app to photo-sharing sites and also to a site called Bing Maps. Bing Maps will display your panorama on a map in the place you took it for others to see, and you can check out all the other panoramas too. There is an app you can pay for called Autostitch Panorama and it is excellent at taking 180° panoramas and putting it all together for you, but Photosynth can do 180° panos as well as 360°. It can do whatever you want! Here's a 180° panorama of the Eiffel Tower from the top right down to our feet!

Shakeitphoto

It'll cost ya!

We love this app for taking old-school Polaroid pictures (Polaroid cameras used to print the pic as soon as it was taken and you could watch it develop on the film). Simply aim your camera as normal and press the shutter button to take the picture. Once the picture is taken, you watch the photo develop before your eyes and you can also shake your phone to make it develop faster. You can adjust the settings of the application to change the format of the picture. All of the photos taken with the app will have the white border around all the pictures. Ask your parents if they remember this from the olden days!

Colorsplash

It'll cost ya!

Take a photo and then Colorsplash converts it to black and white. Then use your fingers like a paintbrush to highlight the parts you want to stay in colour. Photos can look very dramatic and colours can be super-bright against the monochrome background. There is a free version but for this one we recommend buying it as you can use pictures from your camera and convert them. Whereas, with the free one you can only shoot in the app and the pictures are stuck with the effect forever.

✳ **Hipstamatic**

This is the major league favourite among app enthusiasts. This iPhone app offers a variety of lenses, flashes and film for what seems like an endless combination of outcomes. Upload photos directly to **Facebook** or **Flickr** within the app. If you want even more films and effects, then you can buy them separately to add to your arsenal of wizardry within the Hipstamatic app. You can create photos with different vignettes, filters, light and shade and drama. The only downside is that you can't import photos that have already been taken for post-processing; so all photos taken within the app are forever a Hipstamatic photo. A top tip when using the app is to tap the tiny view finder screen so it becomes full screen (then press the screen instead of the yellow button, as the wider screen then becomes the shutter button) and you can have more control over what you are taking because you can see it! This app can be slow and that can be frustrating, but the results are worth it. The different lenses on Hipstamatic can be very effective at colour saturation. Look at these two pictures and see how the picture of the aqueduct is transformed into a richer-toned photo, with the greens and the blues really leaping out at you.

Camera Plus Pro

It'll cost ya!

This is a good app to have on board. It not only has filters, but an anti-shake mechanism, a burst control that allows you to take up to 40 pictures in quick succession, an edit suite for retouching red-eye and brightening/darkening pictures and so on, and a timer for self-portraits — it really is an everything app in one!

TiltShift Generator

It'll cost ya!

This application simulates a tilt-shift lens that tricks your mind into viewing a photo as a miniature scene like a model railroad for example. You have to focus on a linear or elliptical (oval) region in the image and adjust the amount of blur for maximum fake model effect. If you increase colour saturation, contrast or brightness it further enhances the toy model look. There is a similar free version with Instagram, but it isn't quite as good. You can import pictures taken in other apps with filters on and effects and tinker with them in Tiltshift Generator. It isn't just miniature scenes that work well, portraits and still-life can be effective too. Have an experiment — the app has examples you can look at and practice on. Notice the difference between the original photo on the left and the one with the added tilt shift effect on the right? Your eyes do play tricks — it looks like the people on the station forecourt are miniature models.

SAY WHAT?

" All the effects in apps such as Hipstamatic are lazy ways of making any old rubbish look good, that's why they're so popular! It means that literally anyone can make a half-decent image but as ever, content is the most important thing. However, tilt shift is very popular. If used well, it enhances images taken from high vantage points to create a miniaturisation effect. **"**

Ian Boddy,
Photographer

✳ Other pay-for iPhone apps worth a look

◉ **Pic Grunger** was created to give your pictures that grungy rock club look with various levels of grunge that can be layered over pictures from other apps.

◉ **Pro HDR** is better than the iPhone's in-built subtle HDR effect. It takes three or more pictures in all the various exposures and knits them together to produce an impressive HDR photo (see page 12) on such a small device.

◉ **SketchMee** does what it says on the tin! Turns your pictures into a sketch!

◉ **TouchRetouch** allows you to highlight unwanted picture elements with your finger and hit go to make them disappear. Good for people you want out of the picture! Ha!

- **QuickShot with Dropbox** allows you to edit on the hoof and then directly upload your photos to Dropbox online (top remote photo storage facility). Also available for Android.

- **CameraBag** is like Hipstamatic and Instagram — lots of effects.

- **Slow Shutter Cam** for shooting at night lets in more light and measures it all for you taking out the stress.

   And, and, and, and, so many, many more!

Edit suites for iPhones

Editing suites are apps that are a collection of adjustments for brightness, colour and so on. These are the equivalent of laptop photo-editing apps like iPhoto or Photoshop for your iPhone. If you're looking to use one app for all of your photo-editing, these would be a good place to start.

- **Photoshop Express** is very basic but might be all that you need as it isn't complicated. And it's free!

- **Perfect Photo** will cost you and is focused on basic iPhone photographers. It can remove red-eye, fix acne and do a decent amount of basic adjustments.

- Also worth mentioning are **Photogene** and **Iris Photo Suite**, both of these are a lot more complicated and will cost you as well.

REALITY CHECK

☑ Real Photography

Photographer Chase Jarvis said that "The best camera is the one that's with you". This should ring true for the controversial pictures taken on an iPhone of the war in Afghanistan. Damon Winter's photo taken in Hipstamtic made the front page of **The New York Times**, causing outrage that a point-and-press mobile phone picture could command such a prestigious placing. "What about 'real' photography?" people cried.

Maybe this is real photography; lugging a huge camera bag with lenses in isn't going to be safe when you are dodging bullets! Perhaps camera phone photography is the way forward in high-stress situations where a good eye and a reliable piece of equipment is all you need. Now, what did I do with my charger...?

OFFICIAL FORM C-185A

✳ ANDROID APPS

Most of these are pretty much the same as the iPhone apps. As we type, Instagram is being developed for the Android market. Yay! Here are a few we've picked out to try.

The Official Flickr Android app

This app is Instagram for the Android, with filters and effects galore. There is also the ability to upload your photos to the **Flickr** website as well and share online, just like in Instagram. We will explain more about photo-sharing in the next chapter.

Camera360

Camera360 is one of the best free apps for Android. As good, if not better than, Instagram, including an excellent tilt-shift and colour-shift mode. You can also add poster effects, painterly effects, produce HDR photos (see page 12) and more.

Pudding Camera

This app is gaining lots of fans. It is very similar to Instagram and Hipstamatic but has extra features such as a fish-eye lens, self-portrait mode, panorama and loads of cool filters and effects. It has photo-sharing ability and has its own website like Instagram. It is available for the iPhone market as well. And it's free!

Action Snap Pro

It'll cost ya!

With this app, you can create a cool sequence of photos. This allows you to take four or nine photos in a row. Your phone's camera can be configured to combine shots every one to five seconds to form a horizontal photo sequence.

Paper Camera

It'll cost ya!

Real-time cartoon and painting effects displayed with your camera pics. You can even make your own comic book if you want! Why not start a new craze and live your life in a cartoon...?

It'll cost ya!

PicSayPro

This is one of the silliest apps for adding a little something extra to a photo before uploading to Facebook or sending to a friend. You can add props, stickers and speech bubbles which make an ordinary photo hilarious. Well, they are to us...

Camera ZOOM FX

Apparently this is the best Android camera app, according to a lot of people. Everything is on there that isn't on Camera360. You can combine effects in a layer to create multifaceted pictures that will impress.

It'll cost ya!

Other Android apps worth a look

- **Retro Camera** gives you old-style picture effects like Hipstamatic and Instagram. Amazing, and it's free!

- **ColorUp** is free, or pay for the ability to share the photos off your phone. It's the same as iPhone ColorSplash except it doesn't have an undo tool.

- **PicPlz** wants to be Instagram, with similar effects and the ability to post to photo-sharing sites. There's also an Instagram-like activity feed to keep track of people you're following.

- **Instant Camera** takes old-school Polaroid pics like the iPhone Shakeit app.

- **Vignette** has over 100 filters and frames and cool effects. Like Hipstamatic and Instagram in one. There's also a timer and time-lapse feature.

It'll cost ya!

It'll cost ya!

Edit suites for Androids

The Android edit suites are just as good, if not better, than iPhone ones. **Photoshop** is free, totally self-explanatory and the same as the iPhone one. **Picshop** is a free edit suite and ticks the right boxes with all the basic red-eye removal and so on, but also comes with tilt shift and lots of other cool effects. Why pay for one when this is so great?

✳ BLACKBERRY APPS

The Blackberry has hardly any apps available in the UK app store and if you want to download the ones available in the US store, in theory you can as long as it is compatible with your phone. It will say in the blurb if the app is compatible when you click on it to read more information about the one you fancy. There are so many photo apps in the US app store that to list them would be insane, so go check out **appworld.blackberry.com** and click on apps and then search for Photo apps in the search option to the right. The list is endless — top tip, go for the free ones!

However, with or without effects you can take some decent pictures with the cameras on these phones. And post-effects can always be added online if you download onto an edit suite site. Check out the next chapter for online advice and photo-sharing websites with inbuilt edit suites.

GET REAL! Editing snaps from your Blackberry

I have a Blackberry Curve and I use it to take pictures of my friends and on the bus to school. I use apps if they're free and will download them and usually put them on Facebook or edit them in Picasa."

Emily, age 13

(See page 57, for more about Picasa)

REALITY CHECK

 App happy

Photo apps and mobile phone photography are really big business, so maybe you should go out there and invent another app to make your millions? To prove our case, look at some facts:

The human race now takes as many photos every two minutes as the entire world took back in the 1800s. As we said before, step away from photographing what you had for lunch!

The mega-cool app Instagram recently announced that they have grown to over 100 million registered users since their launch in 2010, and have shared over 4 billion photos on their photo-sharing website so far. And a cool 200 million Instagram photos are uploaded to Facebook every day.

As of going to press, there are over ten thousand photo-related apps available out there to try. Now can you see why we can only mention a few of the best? You would still be reading the list when you are old and wrinkly and something better had been invented!

OFFICIAL FORM C-185A

Dude!

Take pictures of any subject, landscape, still-life, whatever takes your fancy. And then try out all the different filters, effects, lenses you can so you can see how different everything looks using various apps. That way, you can get a handle on whether some effects are better suited for still-life, people, landscapes, city scenes, animals, movement, beach scenes, and so on. Instagram is a good place to start as you take the picture and add the effect afterwards. A good measure is to take a close-up picture of a coloured glass bottle and effect it up to the max in all the different lenses and films and see what looks best.

Fast Photo Editor

This one is free but it's not fast! Applying changes can take time. You can rotate, change contrast, resize and much more, but once you have changed the photo, the app doesn't save the original and it can be lost forever if you don't have a duplicate on your camera.

PhotoCard

Another free app, it takes your photos and creates them into a digital 'card'. It's not as cool as it sounds and the end results can be a bit of a let down with the fonts and text, but for free you can't complain too much. The filters are quite good though, a bit like Hipstamatic and Instagram. And, like a postcard, you can send it to your friends via **Twitter**, and **Facebook**! You can also upload and email it.

InstaPhoto

It'll cost ya!

This will cost you but it is better than Fast PhotoEditor and PhotoCard. If you download this you will be getting the Instagram experience for the Blackberry (so you can stop being jealous!). There are lots of cool effects and filters. You can also share directly to Facebook, Twitter and tumblr.

GET REAL!

"All my photos are taken in Hipstamatic. In fact I don't think I ever take a picture that isn't Hipstamatic because I love all the colours, effects and how you can make something ordinary look so cool. Like it was taken years ago on an old fashioned camera."

Martha, 13

QUICK EXPERT SUMMARY

- Effects are amazing and can make your pictures look totally professional, especially if you layer them (take a picture add an effect, save it, then add another effect on top of that) and really experiment.

- Think about what effect you want to create when you take the picture if you are putting the filter on afterwards.

- If you are shooting with the filter or effect instantly, try and set up the shot to maximise this and make it as interesting as possible.

- Most 'raw' original shots, whether they be portrait, landscape, city scene, pet pic – whatever, can be dramatically changed by adding a simple filter or vignette.

53

SHOWING OFF
YOUR WORK

This is the bit of the book where you get to see the end results, people! All that experimenting will not have been in vain. It's now time to print out your pictures so you have a proper copy! Who does that anymore?

CAMERA PHONE FACT

In Moscow in May 2012, journalist Julia Ioffe captured an iconic snap of a little boy facing down a line of riot police on the eve of Vladimir Putin's third term as president. The little boy was on his bike with stabilisers and just scooted off moments later unfazed. Of course the moment of history was taken on a camera phone and beamed around the world pretty much instantly!

* PHOTO SHARING

Social network sites seem to be the most popular places to share your photos with friends and family. And they can be a good way to nosey at what photographers are taking pictures of and how they take them. Glean inspiration for your own pics. If you are on **Facebook** or **Twitter** you will already be familiar with sharing your photos from your phone or iPod Touch. Most smartphones and Blackberries have a Facebook app already in the menu so updating your status has never been easier (or more addictive).

Apps like Instagram, **Flickr** and **tumblr** are similar to Facebook and other social networking sites in that you have to create a profile and you upload your photos to it via the app on your phone when you take a picture. You can log onto the sites from a computer without a profile just to check out the pictures, but if you want to upload and follow people (like on Facebook), you need to create your profile. All these are open-forum sites where people can comment and give you feedback on what you have taken. They are used by photographers as well as mere mortals to showcase their take on the world. If you want to post your photos like an expert, get cracking and create a profile if you haven't already. Then you can see what the competition is up to!

As discussed in the apps section, there are other apps with newsfeed information as well as in-house photo edit suites. New ones are emerging all the time, so we're not going to list all of them here. Get involved and do a search for yourself!

✳ PHOTOBLOGGING

Blogs are also a good way to share photos and show the world what you can do. There is a whole other Quick Expert book on how to create your own blog (**Writing a Blog**) and Tumblr and Instagram are essentially photoblog sites. But you can start a one-off blog that features just your photos about a particular interest or of your daily breakfast (interesting!) for example.

A professional photojournalist posted a blog recording his photos from the London 2012 Olympics using only an iPhone as his camera. It was his experiment to see how accurately he could capture the atmosphere and happenings at the Games without professional equipment. Look here to see how he got on. It is very impressive. **guardian.co.uk/sport/2012/jul/27/london-olympics-2012-smartphone?INTCMP=SRCH**

* DOWNLOAD THOSE WORKS OF ART

Online edit suites are the best way to add effects if you have a very basic phone with no way of downloading photo apps. Most basic phones these days do tend to have an edit suite built into them where you can change the contrast of a picture and add filters and vignettes. But if you want to go online and have a mess around you need to download your pictures from your phone to a laptop or computer. The easiest ways to do this are: Bluetooth them to your laptop (select Bluetooth on your phone settings and switch on the Bluetooth on the computer); use the USB cable that comes with your phone to transfer into your picture files on the laptop; or, if you have the technology on your phone, email them to yourself.

If you have an iPhone or iPod Touch and are syncing your phone to a computer, your phone pictures are automatically imported into iPhoto. Any phone using a USB cable plugged into an Apple Mac computer will have their phone photos automatically downloaded into iPhoto. Check the manual for your phone and see what it says about downloading pictures onto a laptop as each phone is slightly different. The USB cable is really the best way as you can transfer the whole lot instead of one picture at a time. But take a look on the internet and **Google**: 'how to transfer pictures from my *enter name of phone here* to a computer'. There will be video tutorials on sites such as YouTube.

SAY WHAT?

" When you photograph people in colour you photograph their clothes. But when you photograph people in black and white, you photograph their souls! "

**Ted Grant,
Photographer**

Try this quick mini-test before you go for it big time with the end-of-the-book project. Why not try switching your camera phone to black and white and if it doesn't have that setting, go into an app and select black and white. Shoot exclusively in that mode. A lot of photographers have said that if you take away the colour you can concentrate on what you are looking at and can take a very different picture altogether. Give it a go. Then shoot the same picture in colour. Print both of them out and see and feel how each picture is different from the other.

Dude!

✳ ONLINE PICTURE MAGIC

So you have the photos on your computer and now you can apply effects galore. If you are lucky enough to have access to a Mac computer, they have edit suite iPhoto as standard so, lucky you, have a tinker on there! Lots of fun effects and filters. There is a basic suite for PCs called Windows Live Photo Gallery that lets you view your photos in your picture file and edit them in a very basic fashion. But if you want to venture out into the World Wide Web, then take a look at **Picasa** which is owned by Google and is free. Picasa is a type of computer software that allows you to organise and edit digital photographs.

Once downloaded and installed onto the hard drive of your computer (very, very easy, just follow the instructions!), Picasa can be used to view, edit, make collages, track and import digital images that are uploaded onto your computer. It finds your photos for you and you can pick which ones you want to change using effects and filters in the extra Picnik edit suite in the menu. You can also share images with the Picasa web albums feature, which allows photos to be shared with other Google account holders. You can print from the site too, to your computer or via the website for a more professional finish (obviously depending on how cruddy, err amazing, your home printer is...).

Flickr also has an online edit suite called **Aviary** which you can download photos into and tamper with to your heart's content and then upload to the site for sharing. You can also order prints of your photos from here once you have edited them or in their original untampered form.

Paint.NET is also a free edit suite you can download if your computer runs Windows. There are a lot of online edit suites and you can check them out by Googling 'free photo edit suites'. We are just recommending the most used ones. There are of course ones such as **Zenfolio** and **Smugmug** that you can pay for, but what's the point when there is so much free help out there?

QUICK EXPERT SUMMARY

- Start sharing your amazing creations. Get online and use social networking sites and apps such as tumblr to share your photos.

- Download your pictures onto your laptop and start using the free edit suites available to transform your snaps.

- Get printing! We are so used to looking at pictures via a screen that people forget to print their work out. It makes a huge difference to how you feel when you experience the photo's effect on a clean crisp piece of photo paper. Very old-school, but it's what an Expert would do!

THE LAST WORD ON CAMERA PHONE PHOTOGRAPHY

Having **dipped your toe** in the water of phone photography, hopefully you can now **go forth** and take some **amazing pictures** with whatever piece of equipment you may have. The most important thing to remember is **to have fun!**

Tell your own photo story!

Back in the mists of time, people had photo albums where they stuck pictures of what was going on in their lives. These albums would tell a story of a particular event and the colours and energy would bounce off the page. Sometimes looking at photos on a screen can desensitise you to the power of a great photograph because the photo is only ever as vibrant or dramatic as the screen it is on. Nothing can beat holding a bunch of photos in your hand and taking in the reality of them. Oh, we're getting a bit carried away!

So how about you set yourself a little project? Take a load of pics and get them professionally printed out or even better, made into a book or a collage!

Step 1   Choose your subject

Take a subject, any subject (this could be difficult as that implies infinity), like Home, Our Night, Day Out, Frankie's Party (do you know a Frankie? Yes? Freaky!), School Days, Friends, My Mad Family, A Day in My Life, Sports Day, Holiday, anything really that sparks your interest.

Step 2   Start taking those pics

Snap, snap, snap and snap some more, taking into account all the advice you have read here and all the pictures and photo blogs you have hopefully investigated on the net. Think carefully about content, angles, lighting, cropping, framing, movement, textures, emotions and composition (we're not asking much!).

Step 3 | Get printing

Then, when you feel you have covered the subject proficiently, tinkered with ones you want to tinker with, go get them printed-off. They will all have to be in the same place to do this, so ideally on your computer. You will need to select the cream of the crop for this as it could end up costing you a fortune! Sites that are brilliant for printing out your snaps are Kodak Gallery, SnapFish, Blurb and PhotoBox. There are lots out there on the net, but these ones are some of the best. Blurb especially is the site used by professional photographers to make bound photo books to give to clients. You can select photos direct from your computer hard drive but also connect to Facebook and Flikr (SnapFish) as well as Picasa and Instagram (Blurb) and grab photos from there. A cheaper option, if you have a photo printer at home, is to print off your pics from there.

Step 4 | Create a photo book

You could design a bound book rather than putting the pictures in an album, but you'll have to design it all yourself! Blurb and Snapfish are great, as is Kodak Gallery. If you have access to a Mac and iPhoto you can turn your snaps from your gallery into proper photo books that you then order from the online store. Again, you have to do all the hard work designing!

Step 5 | Admire your handiwork

All photos/books have to be paid for online and then a while later you will be the proud owner of a photo book made entirely by you. Whether it is bound and printed by the site or you bought the album and stuck them in, you did it. Notice how different it is printing them out rather than looking at them via a screen. It is better, we think...

aperture — the adjustable hole inside a camera lens that lets the light in to hit the sensor on a Digital SLR camera

backlighting — a light placed behind the subject you are photographing

blog — a discussion or informational site published on the World Wide Web and consisting of entries (posts) usually displayed in reverse chronological order (the most recent post appears first)

bokeh — the quality of blurring in a photograph

depth of field — a measure of how much of a scene (from the front to the back of the image) will be in focus

digital zoom — the button on a DSLR or ordinary digital camera that allows you to zoom closer to your subject, enlarging it while still appearing as a sharp image

exposure — refers to the light sensor in a digital camera (or film in a traditional camera) being exposed to light through a combination of shutter speed and aperture size

film — light-sensitive material that is used instead of an image sensor in traditional cameras.

filter — in traditional photography, a gel-like film placed directly over the camera lens to change the colour or atmosphere of the picture

HDR — High Dynamic Range. The camera takes two or more photos of the same thing using different exposures and then 'knits' them together, capturing all the different tones and light and shade.

histogram — a graph that shows all the measurements of where and how much light and shade appear in a digital photograph

image sensor — a device behind the lens that converts the light coming through the lens into an electronic signal ready to be processed into an image by the camera's computer

lens — typically made of glass, but some can be made of plastic. The lens makes the picture in a camera by capturing the light reflected off the subject and focusing it onto the film or sensor to create the image.

lens flare — when you point the camera directly into the sun or light source and get a halo effect bouncing off the subject

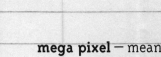

mega pixel — meaning a million pixels, which is a measurement of the pixels (dots) on the camera sensor

noise — the small coloured spots in the dark parts of a digital photograph

panning — when you move the camera steadily, tracking your subject and taking pictures as you go

panorama — a 180° (sometimes 360°) photograph of a scene, capturing the entire horizon in front of you

pixel — a tiny dot in a digital photograph. Thousands of these dots make up a digital picture.

Polaroid — clunky old-school instant camera with the classic thick white border framing the photo

red-eye — when the subject's eyes in the picture are red, caused by the flash illuminating the retina at the back of the eye

resolution — the actual measurement of the mega pixels on the camera sensor or pixel measurement on a digital photograph

rule of thirds — a standard photography composition term whereby you divide the scene you are shooting into thirds horizontally and vertically and place the subject in one of the thirds other than in the centre

shutter — a device in cameras that opens for a certain amount of time to let light come in through the aperture on the lens and expose the photographic film or sensor to the light

SLR/DSLR — Single Lens Reflex and Digital SLR. Means the view you see directly through the lens is exactly what will appear on your photograph.

spot focus — keeping just one tiny spot of the photograph in focus

tilt shift — a picture that is an optical illusion through the manipulation of focus, making pictures from a distance resemble miniature models

toy cameras — the name given to a whole group of fun, cheap cameras made from plastic (including the lens), creating bright pictures and all sorts of effects replicated in photo apps

vignette — the blurring or burnt-out framing around the edge of photos; you can create this when using an app, which has a similar effect to a toy camera photo

>>> INDEX <<<